An Animal Fa

SEALS AND PUPS

By Emilia Hendrix

Gareth Stevens
PUBLISHING

Please visit our website, www.garethstevens.com. For a free color catalog of all our high-quality books, call toll free 1-800-542-2595 or fax 1-877-542-2596.

Library of Congress Cataloging-in-Publication Data

Hendrix, Emilia, author.
 Seals and pups / Emilia Hendrix.
     pages cm. — (An animal family)
 Includes index.
 ISBN 978-1-4824-3787-4 (pbk.)
 ISBN 978-1-4824-3788-1 (6 pack)
 ISBN 978-1-4824-3789-8 (library binding)
 1. Seals (Animals)—Juvenile literature. 2. Seals (Animals)—Behavior—Juvenile literature. I. Title.
 QL737.P6H46 2016
 599.79—dc23

                                   2015025060

First Edition

Published in 2016 by
Gareth Stevens Publishing
111 East 14th Street, Suite 349
New York, NY 10003

Copyright © 2016 Gareth Stevens Publishing

Editor: Ryan Nagelhout
Designer: Andrea Davison-Bartolotta

Photo credits: Cover, p. 1 Mariusz Potocki/Shutterstock.com; p. 5 zaferkizilkaya/Shutterstock.com; p. 7 Dave Turner/Shutterstock.com; p. 9 Benoit Daoust/Shutterstock.com; pp. 11, 23, 24 (pup) Dmytro Pylypenko/ Shutterstock.com; p. 13 Peter Chadwick/Getty Images; p. 15 Stephan Morris/Shutterstock.com; p. 17 Dimos/ Shutterstock.com; p. 19 Richard Herrmann/Getty Images; pp. 21, 24 (colony) davide guidolin/Shutterstock.com.

Printed in the United States of America

CPSIA compliance information: Batch #CW16GS: For further information contact Gareth Stevens, New York, New York at 1-800-542-2595.

Contents

Seals live in the sea.

They also live on land.

Seals love to swim!

Baby seals are called pups.

Pups love to play.

They stay close
to their mother.

Their mother brings them food.

Seals eat lots of fish.

A group of seals is
called a colony.

A colony can be loud!

Words to Know

colony

pup

Index